TREE HUGGING

---- POCKET NATURE ----

Seek Wisdom in the Forest

By Gregory Han and Emily Han

Cover Art by Andrea Serio
Interior Illustrations by Liana Jegers

---- POCKET NATURE ----

TREE
HUGGING

CHRONICLE BOOKS
SAN FRANCISCO

POCKET NATURE SERIES

Text copyright © 2025 by **GREGORY HAN** and **EMILY HAN**.

All rights reserved. No part of this book may be reproduced in any form without written permission from the publisher.

Library of Congress Cataloging-in-Publication Data available.

ISBN 978-1-7972-3421-2

Manufactured in China.

Series concept and editing by **CLAIRE GILHULY**.
Series design by **LIZZIE VAUGHAN**.
Typesetting by **NGHI TO**.
Cover art by **ANDREA SERIO**.
Interior illustrations by **LIANA JEGERS**.
Typeset in Albra, Benton Sans, Caslon.

10 9 8 7 6 5 4 3 2 1

Chronicle books and gifts are available at special quantity discounts to corporations, professional associations, literacy programs, and other organizations. For details and discount information, please contact our premiums department at corporatesales@chroniclebooks.com or at 1-800-759-0190.

Chronicle Books LLC
680 Second Street
San Francisco, California 94107
www.chroniclebooks.com

For Grandma & Grandpa Warren,
*whose voices resonate
among the birds and branches.*

CONTENTS

INTRODUCTION 9

I.
What Makes a Tree a Tree? 15

II.
How Trees Nurture Connections 55

III.
The Wisdom of Trees 85

RESOURCES 110

Trees are POEMS
that the EARTH
writes upon THE SKY.

—Kahlil Gibran, from *Sand and Foam*

INTRODUCTION

Just a few inches beneath the surface in a light-dappled clearing, something miraculous is about to unfold. Out of the thousands of acorns methodically stashed along the forest floor by an industrious squirrel, the tough, leathery shell of a single nut begins to stir. Awakened by a steady rain and dampened soil, the slumbering acorn starts to crack along the smooth, tapered end. Soon after, like a ladybug readying for flight, each half of the acorn's lacquered shell slowly pushes farther apart. A glimpse of pale yellow within gives way to the appearance of a ghostly taproot that anchors into the earth. Uncoiling from their shell, the seedling emerges; yearning for air and sunlight, their first leaves unfurl like small sails.

Even if this sprout is fortunate enough to survive the appetites of foraging deer and insects, outliving other nearby saplings during their first few years, it will be several decades before the tree reaches full maturity. As their roots, trunk, and branches stretch across soil and sky, the oak will join their arboreal ancestors in a literal family tree. On average, only one in several thousand acorns grows into a tree, making every oak you've ever encountered a minor miracle.

Our desire to live alongside these wonders drew the two of us to our current home, a residence enveloped by five oak trees and defined by the adjacent riparian woodland. Though we each grew up in different ecosystems, both of us counted trees among our favorite childhood companions. From the coast live oaks and western sycamores of Southern California to the live oaks, pecans, and mesquites of South Texas, these trees imprinted upon us a sense of both familiarity and awe. Today, we lead busy lives as writers and educators in the fields of design and technology, landscape architecture, herbal medicine, and nature connection. Still, we always make time to seek the counsel of trees and the web of life they support.

When strolling in the nearby woods, we also delight in seeing the ways that children interact with the trees. To a child, a tree is rarely *only* a tree. A tree extends deep into our imaginations, entangled with our earliest fantasies, while rooting our purest hopes. Silent and agreeable, a tree easily assumes the role of a pal and confidant, castle tower, rocket ship, and nearly anything a youthful mind can conjure. We swing from a tree's limbs, hide behind their trunk, and rest in their cool shadow. While dangling upside down from a branch or drawing our first trees with crayons, we find new perspectives. In the process of play, a tree's vibrant community comes to light: a bird's nest tucked in a hollow, a family of chipmunks scurrying across the roots, our cautious curiosity stirred when hearing the thrum of bees emanating from a trunk, the intriguing oddities underneath logs.

As we become older, a tree takes on additional layers of meaning. We bury loved ones beneath their canopy or plant saplings in remembrance. The weathered countenance of bark paired with the optimism of spring's earliest leaves become symbolic of our own growing and aging families. It's no surprise we are apt to love a tree like a dear friend or family member, their presence a comforting reminder of our own growth, loss, and renewal.

Yet, in our everyday lives, trees can fade into the background. We might consider ourselves admirers of trees, marveling at them during certain times of year or when we travel to visit special places, such as viewing plum blossoms in spring or a blaze of foliage in autumn. But outside of this intent to "escape to nature," a kind of indifference is normalized. As we commute to work, grab a coffee in town (made from the fruit of trees), or even find relief in a tree's shade, we frequently take for granted the trees that are already part of our lives.

How well do you know the trees outside your doorstep? Who was the last tree you really spent time with? Can you recall their particular textures, shapes, sounds, scents, or colors? Did you pause to give them a hug? In the chapters that follow, we hope to kindle a sense of curiosity and wonder as we explore the nature of trees, the interconnected relationships they nurture, and the wisdom we can learn when we slow down to really appreciate a tree.

Cheerful cheerful
the old tree
BEFRIENDS the
YOUNG leaves.

—**Kobayashi Issa** (translated by Stephen Addiss)

I.

WHAT MAKES A TREE A TREE?

It is a brisk, early Sunday morning when the two of us begin tracing our footsteps along a favorite local trail. A swath of marine layer slipped its way inland the night before, enveloping the land in a gray silence that greets those motivated enough to awaken ahead of the birdsong. Only in the early afternoon, at the insistence of the sun, will the atmospheric grip of cool air finally loosen. But for hikers, there may be no better time to be amongst the trees than during these hours of stillness.

Our backyard overlooks this length of riparian habitat along the foothills of the Angeles National Forest, Tongva land. Barely discernible when viewed from above, the trail is enveloped by a dense canopy of trees supported by a spring-fed creek. From such a vantage point, the treetops can look like a crowd during a sold-out concert, each individual only partially discernible from another. Sometimes, like concertgoers, they even sway in unison.

But from the ground level, our perception changes considerably. Only a few minutes into our walk, we find ourselves in the dampened embrace of a contorting network of coast live oak branches, a popular highway for gray squirrels. California bay trees perfume the air, scented before sighted. Elongated clusters of greenish-yellow alder flowers, called *catkins*, confetti the path underfoot. The mottled white and tan trunks of western sycamores peek through with pale clarity against the lush backdrop of green foliage following the creek. Our senses inform us that we are amongst a diversity of beings both individually and communally in relationship with the land.

WHAT IS A TREE?

Trees are everywhere, defining the landscape both in their presence and absence. But how did they get here? Before we seek the answer to *how*, we need to address the *what*—as in, what exactly makes a tree a tree? This deceptively simple question opens up a world of fascinating and complex natural history.

A tree can be defined as a tall, perennial (living more than two years) plant with a woody structure. Or as *Elderflora* author Jared Farmer succinctly explains, "Trees are plants that people call trees—a term of dignity, not botany." Trees do typically have a single main stem, or trunk, from which a network of branches and leaves grows. Unlike shrubs with their multiple stems and low-lying stature, trees seem to have higher aspirations in their quest for sunlight.

However, it isn't the height nor the woody structure that solely satisfies the definition of what makes a tree. At their full height, least

willows measure only a few inches tall, yet many consider them trees (the world's smallest, in fact). Some plants we think of as trees, like Joshua trees and fan palms, may not even really be trees at all (Joshua trees are succulents, and some botanists note that palms are more closely related to grasses than to typical trees). The differentiation between trees and other plants can be arbitrary, with cultural perceptions as influential as any botanical distinctions.

HOW TREES CAME TO BE AND BRANCHED OUT

We might assume trees have always been part of our landscape, but their story spans hundreds of millions of years, rife with opportunistic twists, adaptive turns, and branched dead ends—not unlike the morphology of trees themselves. If we imagine traveling back about 500 million years, we might at first be pleasantly surprised by the accommodating mild temperature. But we'd quickly realize the planet was devoid of any significant expanse of vegetation, let alone anything remotely resembling trees (not to mention breathable air). Plants had only recently emerged from a life aquatic, growing to heights measured in mere centimeters. Within the next 70 million years or so, creeping and crawling arachnids, centipedes, and millipedes began to appear, long before dinosaurs wandered the Earth. Life on land was only just getting started, offering an ankle-high safari at best.

Without complex roots, stems, and leaves, early plants had to rely upon damp environments to survive (much like most mosses today). Then, about 390 million years ago, plants developed softwood trunks resembling modern conifers like pine trees. This was a transformative version 2.0 upgrade, giving plants structural support so they could anchor themselves to the soil, grow taller, and stay hydrated. As they continued to adapt to life in soil, plants like ferns and horsetails also emerged, giving safe cover to the first vertebrates who evolved with four limbs and crawled out from water onto dry land. Among the earliest known trees are *Archaeopteris*, whose fossils have been found on every continent, including Antarctica. These ancient trees reached heights of nearly 100 feet [30 m] with trunks measuring over 3 feet [1 m] in diameter.

Spreading to cover the globe, these and other ancestral trees fundamentally altered the soil and water and pulled carbon dioxide from the atmosphere while increasing the percentage of oxygen—creating the ecology of the world we now inhabit. Over millennia, trees would evolve into the approximately seventy-three thousand species on Earth today. Some, like the ginkgo and Wollemi pine, have remained relatively unchanged for hundreds of millions of years, making them living fossils among us.

Those tens of thousands of tree species express an enormous diversity of shapes and sizes, from the towering redwoods of the Pacific Northwest to the largest contiguous mangrove forest in Bangladesh. Trees and their environments are engaged in a continuous reciprocity, each shaping and being shaped by the other. To know a tree is to also know a place. Stored in a tree's roots, trunk, and canopy is a physical record and arboreal memoir quietly telling what has transpired in that specific location across generations of time.

Roots: Notes from the Underground

Beneath the soil's surface, out of sight and often out of mind, lies one of the most remarkable parts of a tree: their root system. But roots are generally underappreciated, if not viewed with a bit of antagonism in the context of our built landscape; they can intrude into our pipes, push up sidewalks, and complicate the plans of determined gardeners. But considered in context of an adaptation, these all highlight the impressive strength trees have evolved to not only survive, but thrive, with roots as their foundational support.

We can also admire a tree's roots for their near-unassailable resolve to gather water and nourishment from the soil and store food for the future. A tree is rooted in place, but those roots extend themselves over impressive distances and obstacles to raid the underground pantry. At once strong and intricate, root systems consist of larger, longer-lived roots as well as shorter-lived feeder roots and root hairs, which are sometimes microscopically fine. A tree's footprint often extends much wider than we might think; oak and maple roots can spread up to three times the radius of the crown. Roots can grow a few feet deep or, like the natal fig, plow down to depths of 400 feet [122 m] below the surface—approximately half the length of the *Titanic*.

In addition to water, roots respond to their environment to draw up nutrients, minerals, and oxygen in the soil. Each tree has evolved for a particular kind of soil, from waterlogged swamps to rocky cliffs. To forage for water and nutrients, roots follow channels in the soil, fissures in rocks, tunnels made by worms, and yes, occasionally your home's plumbing. As they weave among the roots of other trees and plants, they also interact with a multiplicity of beings, including insects, fungi, and bacteria.

Roots can exhibit extraordinary strength, prying and breaking apart rocks and in the process making nutrients more available for use by other plants and animals. Some trees' roots are so industrious, they actively "mine" the soil by producing chemicals that dissolve minerals. Other trees redistribute the water they find. Longleaf pine and sugar maple, for instance, pull up groundwater with their deep roots during the day, and then at night, they release moisture into the shallow soil, where it can be absorbed by their feeder roots and other nearby plants.

All of this activity helps shape a tree's surroundings. Roots can hold soil in place and prevent water and wind from washing it away, particularly along riverbanks and on slopes. They can also catch sediment, causing soil to build up. Where the two of us live, this relationship is pronounced at the curves of local creeks and alongside precipitous canyon walls, where oak trees cling with a muscular confidence. Like a potter at the wheel, over the span of generations and through the accumulation of soil and the grip of their roots, these trees have sculpted their surroundings, influencing how water flows from the mountains to the foothills to the sea.

Roots typically delve underground, but some habitats call for other strategies. In coastal swamps where the land is saturated with water and the soil is loose and oxygen-poor, mangrove trees grow aboveground roots that resemble stilts and buttresses. As the tides ebb and flow, these uplifted root systems assist in filtering out salts and obtaining oxygen. By slowing the water flow, mangrove roots also prevent erosion and create rich habitats for crabs, anemones, fish, and other aquatic and shoreline creatures.

We may never get to see all the intricacies of a tree's root system, but being aware of its presence can help us better understand the entirety of a tree's reach.

TREE HUGGING

ELEMENTAL RELATIONSHIPS

Wood may be a defining element of trees, but trees also embody and interact with the elements of fire, earth, air, and water. Here are four exemplars:

Manzanita *(Arctostaphylos* spp.*)* ▶ **FIRE**
Manzanita trees' connection to fire goes beyond the reddish-orange color of their bark. For millions of years, periodic fires have shaped the chaparral ecosystems where manzanitas live. Although most manzanitas succumb to the flames, their seeds, lying dormant in the soil, often require fire to germinate. Researchers believe chemicals in smoke or burned wood catalyze these seeds to sprout.

Mesquite *(Prosopis* spp.*)* ▶ **EARTH**
Aboveground, mesquite trees are distinguished by their graceful leaves and nutritious seedpods. Belowground, mesquites are adapted for dry soils and can plunge their long taproots deep into the earth—up to 200 feet [61 m]—in search of water. Their shallower roots also partner with fungi and

nitrogen-fixing bacteria, enhancing the availability of nutrients and transforming the land around them.

Banyan *(Ficus benghalensis)* ▶ **AIR**
Life begins in the air when a bird or other animal plops a banyan seed in the crown of another tree. The seedling has all they need from sunlight, moisture, and nutrients they pull from decaying plant matter. As roots reach toward the ground, these distinctive aerial structures eventually engulf the host tree, leading to the nickname of "strangler fig." A mature banyan's canopy can provide ample shade; India's sacred Thimmamma Marrimanu tree covers nearly five acres!

Willow *(Salix* spp.*)* ▶ **WATER**
You'll typically find willows growing in wetlands and moist soils. Amidst the turbulence of flowing water, their shallow roots grasp the soil, preventing erosion. In addition to providing food for animals, willows offer shelter to water beetles, fish, and other aquatic life. Alongside wind, water is integral to willow's reproduction, carrying the tree's fluffy seeds to new locales.

The Trunk: A Pillar of Strength

Though trees seem still, a lot is happening inside. After the roots gather water and nutrients, specialized tissues in the trunk channel it up to the leaves. Meanwhile, the trunk provides structure and support for the crown and leaves. Food made by the leaves flows through the trunk to the rest of the tree to bolster growth or be stored in the roots. (This food takes the form of sugary sap, maple syrup being a familiar example.)

Bearing the marks of time, a tree's waterproof outer bark insulates and protects them from injury. Each tree has their own unique bark, but why are there such different types? When most of us envision a tree growing, we think of them reaching upward. But trees also grow layer by layer, from the inside out, putting pressure against the outer bark. It's a process that directly influences the bark's appearance. If a tree grows slowly, the outer bark has time to expand and accommodate the wood beneath, leaving it smooth. But if a tree swells quickly, they are confronted with a situation similar to our own when we try to squeeze into a too-small pair of denim: an uncomfortably tight fit. A tree doesn't have a top button to loosen, but they can adapt. As a tree matures, they grow the equivalent of roomier and stretchier new jeans underneath, pushing the older fit outward and resulting in a scaly, furrowed, or even cracked texture. On some trees, like shagbark hickory or crape myrtle, the older layers of bark shed or peel off like an exfoliation.

While the majority of trees have bark in tones of brown or gray, some trunks are more conspicuous, having evolved colors for protection. For instance, white bark allows silver birch trees to reflect sunlight and possibly prevent damage from winter temperature changes. The red of madrone bark comes from tannins, protecting the smooth-skinned trees from insects and bacteria. Palo verde trees drop their leaves during drought, but their chlorophyll-laden lime-green bark continues to carry out photosynthesis.

Certain trees protect themselves against herbivores by growing thorns, spines, or prickles on their trunks or branches. The tree we encounter today is the result of numerous adaptations in response to the environment long ago. In the case of the silk floss tree, their prickly presence evolved to deter the enormous appetites of now-extinct megafauna like giant sloths. Beyond defense, thorns may help provide extra shade to trees who live in arid habitats.

Bark can also protect trees in the face of fire. In ecosystems that have evolved with fire, species such as oak, pine, larch, and sequoia have developed thick bark that can help them withstand flames. Other trees, like eucalyptus, have dormant buds under their bark that can sprout after a fire. Redwood trees have even sprouted from thousand-year-old dormant buds. In another adaptation, some conifers and eucalyptus depend on the heat of a wildfire for their cones or fruits to release seeds.

Many trees produce chemicals to protect their trunks, and we might encounter these as stickiness or scent. Like a glass of wine for an oenophile, smelling a tree can awaken vivid associations and memories. You can't tip a tree trunk like a glass of wine, but if you bring your nose up close to a ponderosa pine or Jeffrey pine tree on a warm day, you'll likely smell vanilla or butterscotch. Black cherry bark exudes a bitter-almond aroma that deters herbivores. Conifers often have sticky, fragrant resin that traps insects and protects against infection when the tree is wounded. (For that reason, it's important not to remove resin from an affected area of a trunk.)

Next time you visit a tree, notice the look, feel, or scent of their outer bark. Would you describe it as smooth, rough, ridged, plated, peeling, cracking, papery, knobby?

A Crowning Achievement

It can become a habit to glance over trees as just a wall of green in the background. But when we spend time with an individual tree, we realize how each one is distinct from their neighbors—in size, shape, and of course, the

leaves that make up their crown. As the roots draw sustenance from the soil and water, the crown (or canopy) gathers nourishment from the sun and air. Here, branches and twigs not only support the leaves (as well as flowers, fruit, and seeds); they also extend them toward the light and help transport water and nutrients between the trunk and the leaves.

The world's trees boast a rich variety of leaves—perhaps even more so than the diversity of bark. These can be as small as a spruce tree's 0.4-inch- [10-mm-] long needles, or as colossal as *Coccoloba gigantifolia*'s leaves that exceed the heights of the tallest NBA players. The range of shapes is considerable, from tamarind's crown of feathery leaflets to monkey puzzle's pointed spiral formations. A tree may have thousands or even millions of leaves that carry out photosynthesis, each absorbing sunlight and carbon dioxide from the atmosphere. With these building blocks, alongside water drawn up from the roots, the tree makes food in the form of sugars. In the process, the leaves release oxygen into the air we breathe.

How many varied shapes, sizes, textures, or colors of leaves can you observe in your local park or on your street? These diverse characteristics can determine how well a tree absorbs sunlight and carbon dioxide, conserves moisture, and wards off hungry creatures.

GET TO KNOW A TREE

Seldom do we stop to acknowledge trees as we pass them by. Here's a practice to help you meet a tree more closely. Choose a tree—one who calls out to you for some reason, or even whom you've previously ignored. Approach them with openness and curiosity. Introduce yourself and sit, stand, or lie down near your tree.

(As you do this activity, feel free to modify it to suit your own sensory abilities and sensitivities. You can do all aspects of the exercise or choose a certain sense to focus on. Also, be mindful of not directly touching poisonous trees.)

Spend some time integrating all that you notice and give thanks to the tree for being part of this sensory experience.

- **SIGHT**
  Follow a tree's roots, trunk, or branches as they invite your gaze to shoot upward, meander outward, or bend toward the ground. What kind of silhouette does the crown make against the sky? Do you see colors, light, shadow, or how branches and leaves shape the space around them?

- **HEARING**
  Listen to the sounds on and around the tree. Do you hear wind rustling, raindrops scattering through the canopy, or a crunch of leaves underfoot? Are there any animal sounds?

- **SMELL**
  Take a deep breath and inhale the scent of the tree and the surrounding air and soil. Don't be shy about putting your nose up to the trunk or leaves. Scent can be closely linked to other sensations; do any taste or memory connections arise?

- **TOUCH**
  Feel the textures of the tree. Lean against the trunk, put your palm on the bark, or run your fingers along the edges of a leaf. Do you detect any other sensations on your skin, such as warm sun, cool shade, moisture, or breeze?

FIELD GUIDE

BROADLEAF TREES

Broadleaf trees have flat leaves in various shapes and arrangements. Have you ever noticed that trees growing in shade commonly have larger leaves than trees in full sun? That's because broader leaves can absorb more light. On the other hand, small leaves and compound leaves (leaves made up of smaller leaflets) are less susceptible to evaporation and help a tree conserve moisture. Other adaptations of broadleaves include waxy, waterproof leaves; coarse, leathery leaves that minimize evaporation; lobed edges that lessen wind resistance; hairy surfaces that reflect bright light; and spines that reduce water loss and deter grazing animals. Broadleaf trees produce flowers and fruits and are regularly referred to as *hardwoods*.

CONIFERS

Conifers generally have needle- or scale-like leaves adapted for harsh conditions, like high elevations and colder, drier climates. The thin leaf shape prevents water loss and has lower wind resistance. A waxy coating on the leaves helps conserve moisture when a tree can't take up water from frozen soil. Conifers produce cones instead of flowers and may be referred to as *softwoods*.

DECIDUOUS

Deciduous trees shed their leaves when climate conditions aren't favorable. To conserve energy, these trees stop producing the chlorophyll that turns their leaves green, leaving behind the chemicals that make them appear orange, yellow, red, or purple. In temperate regions, a "turning of the leaves" characterizes the life cycle of autumn-deciduous trees including aspens, maples, and rowans. Their leaves change color, sometimes in dramatic fashion, before being dropped for a period of winter dormancy. When daylight increases again in spring, new leaves and flowers reemerge. Other trees can become deciduous during dry seasons. Drought-deciduous trees like ʻohe makai and desert ironwood let go of their leaves during summer and renew them when moisture returns.

EVERGREEN

Evergreen trees keep their leaves, giving them the ability to photosynthesize year-round. These trees frequently live in warm places, but they can also live in harsh climates where it would take more energy to shed and grow new leaves every year than to simply hold onto them. Examples include hot and dry Mediterranean climates, boreal forests, and tropical and sandy habitats where there isn't enough nutrition in the soil to support frequent leaf growth.

. . .

Like all organisms, trees experience natural rhythms of growth, reproduction, decay, and interactions with their environment. Trees don't have smartphone notifications telling them when it's time to wake up or rest. Instead, because sunlight is so essential to photosynthesis, trees are highly sensitive to changes in light. They follow a diurnal rhythm, synced to the daily patterns of light and darkness (though they're being increasingly disrupted by urban light and climate change). During the day, trees engage in photosynthesis, producing and storing the energy they need to survive. At night, many reserve their energy and enter a restful state, sipping on the sugars produced during the day to sustain themselves.

This night-and-day rhythm can be mirrored on a larger scale by annual or seasonal cycles. For many people, an awareness of these rhythms provides a sense of anticipation as well as comfort.

Sunlight and the elements not only affect the shapes and life cycles of leaves; they can also affect the overall appearance of a tree's crown. Rounded treetops can absorb sunlight from several directions, while flat canopies are often located near the equator where sunlight bears down from directly overhead. Trees become more conical as you move closer to the Arctic Circle where the sun is low. Next time you observe a tree leaning one way or another, contemplate how this might reveal something about the availability of sunlight or intensity of the wind over time.

Besides leaves, the canopy is where we find flowers, fruits, and seeds, which ignite our curiosity with their array of colors, shapes, scents, textures, and tastes. Flowering trees, such as mulberry and chestnut, develop seeds enclosed by an ovary or fruit. Non-flowering trees, including juniper and pine, have "naked seeds," usually within cones. Like the roots, trunk, and leaves, these reproductive structures are adapted to a tree's surroundings. Some trees rely on wind or water to disperse their pollen and seeds, and others have evolved flowers and fruits that entice animals to help in reproduction. Even flowers and fruits that we don't consider edible or pleasant to our senses can be a vital food source for other animals and play an important role in the health of their native ecosystems.

A tree's crown can also have profound effects on the landscape. Like roots, canopies help prevent erosion. They do this by slowing down rainfall hitting the ground or acting as windbreakers. The soil beneath reveals another way trees influence their environment. All that pleasurably crunchy or sodden organic matter consisting of fallen leaves, branches, and bark decomposes with time, adding essential nutrients back into the ground and providing an abundant habitat for fungi, insects, birds, foraging mammals, and others to hide, feed, and reproduce.

And let us not forget the coolness created by a tree's cover and, more subtly, through the act of respiration (yes, trees breathe too). A single tree creates a microclimate; trees in great numbers operate as a large-scale thermostat, lowering surface and air temperatures by providing shade and cooling through evaporation and transpiration, in a process known as *evapotranspiration*. In a study of six hundred cities, researchers found that trees cooled neighborhoods an average of 1.8°F [1.1°C] and up to 5.2°F [2.9°C].

All trees, rainforests especially, are also integral to our planet's water cycle. As trees release moisture back into the atmosphere, this contributes to the formation of clouds and rain, which then falls back to Earth to become groundwater, eventually looping back again.

Which brings us back to the question: What makes a tree a tree? While a tree is physically wood, roots, trunk, and crown and embodies the cycles of soil, air, water, light, and fire, they are also the lineage of their ancestors and the ongoing life of the place they inhabit. A tree is your breath, as you are a tree's breath.

To <u>LISTEN</u> to trees, nature's great <u>CONNECTORS</u>, is therefore to learn how to inhabit the <u>RELATIONSHIPS</u> that give life its <u>SOURCE</u>, <u>SUBSTANCE</u>, and <u>BEAUTY</u>.

—David George Haskell, from *The Songs of Trees*

II.

HOW TREES NURTURE CONNECTIONS

Imagine the world as a grand symphony. Where do you consider yourself in this planetary performance? We may be inclined to envision ourselves as something of a virtuoso or even the conductor. In reality, we are but one member of a vast orchestra. Trees are there too, steadily strumming the underlying notes out of which emerge countless harmonies and even dissonances shared between plants, fungi, animals, and microbes. From their deepest roots to their loftiest branches, a tree quietly hums into the soil and intones into the sky a multiverse of music about everything—the living, dying, reproducing, growing, shedding, renewing—happening all at once.

In both life and death, trees become entwined with a myriad of connections so vital that we have given some trees the honorific of keystone species: the glue that holds an entire ecosystem together. Within this web of life, trees also reap the benefits of these reciprocal partnerships. Sadly, this song of interdependence can escape our notice as we get lost in the minutiae of our lives. Spending time with a tree is an invitation to marvel at the biodiversity that surrounds us. Here are some of the fascinating relationships trees have with other life.

PLANTS

When you sit or stand beside a tree, take a minute to observe your immediate surroundings. Do you detect any patches of sunlight and shadow or shifts in temperature, humidity, and airflow?

Feel the soil. Are any of these qualities different from areas beyond the tree's reach? Trees, especially in groups, can create microclimates where various other plants thrive or struggle. Whether in a dense forest, arid desert, or urban park, see if you come upon any undergrowth of smaller trees, shrubs, herbaceous plants, climbing vines, or tiny mosses. Within a forest, this is known as the understory. In cultivated settings, garden plants may share space. Even on a city curb, volunteer plants (pejoratively known as *weeds*) are common.

Look up as well—some trees sustain other plant life within their crowns, where *epiphytes*, or air plants, glean water and nutrients from the atmosphere. Among oaks and cypress trees in subtropical regions, *Tillandsia* species drape themselves in such a way over branches they can appear like disheveled birds' nests or forgotten clumps of holiday tinsel. (When they fall, these plants contribute to soil fertility.) Meanwhile, the tall branches of tropical ceiba trees host an aerial community that includes blooming bromeliads and squirming apostrophes of tadpoles in water-filled hollows. And high up in redwood canopies, leather leaf ferns form extensive mats, providing moisture and nutrients to the tree and creating microhabitats for insects and salamanders to call home.

Compared to a single tree, a group of trees can substantially alter their surroundings, fostering a multilayered ecosystem of plants, animals, and other beings all interacting. An individual tree can affect weather, landscape, and biodiversity, but, like a chorus, a thriving forest magnifies these influences exponentially. In English, we have numerous collective nouns for animals: a rhumba of rattlesnakes, covey of quail, and skulk of foxes are a few of the more delightful terms. However, our descriptors for tree communities are rather limited to words like *forest*, *woods*, *grove*, *copse*, and *stand*. Many languages and dialects around the world once had vibrant descriptions for groups of trees, but those words have disappeared or are disappearing alongside trees themselves.

Trees and plants typically mingle. But in some forests, you might look up to the highest layer of foliage, or overstory, and notice a peculiar sight: treetops covering the sky but never quite touching, as if each agreed to stay within their bounds. This phenomenon, called *crown shyness*, can occur between trees of the same species or different species, perhaps the result of "pruning" by the wind. The space between canopies may also help reduce wind resistance, improve access to sunlight, and prevent the spread of disease.

Just as a tree's interactions can happen visibly above us, they are also happening below. Sometimes, due to shade or other factors, you may note little else growing near a tree, or only specific native plants who have coevolved with certain trees. Trees like black walnut and tree of heaven engage in *allelopathy*, a release of chemicals into the soil that influences (and often inhibits) the growth of neighboring plants. It's fascinating to investigate which plants manage to coexist and even thrive in their midst—something we personally watched and tested while gardening in a hillside corner populated by Southern California black walnuts.

Touching or not, trees can connect with each other through the air and soil. Roots of separate trees have been known to graft together, facilitating the transfer of water or sugars between trees and even leafless stumps. Some trees pump out distress pheromones when an animal such as a caterpillar or giraffe nibbles on their leaves, prompting nearby trees to fortify their own leaves with unpleasant-tasting chemicals like tannins. Such examples could just be the tip of the leaf when it comes to how trees interact. Researchers are only beginning to unravel other possible communication methods between trees, including electrical signals, sound vibrations, and more.

FUNGI AND LICHENS

As you embark on your scavenger hunt for tree relationships, keep an eye out for the strange and wonderful morphologies, colors, textures, and scents of mushrooms—the fruiting bodies of fungi. You might find mushrooms growing among fallen leaves, sprouting from trunks or stumps, or encircling trees in fairy rings. You may have heard about the "wood wide web," a popularized theory that posits trees share resources and even information via an underground fungal network. Though the idea is currently in heated debate, there's no argument that fungi do often play a pivotal role in the life (and death) of trees, forming hidden connections underfoot.

Since the earliest days of their evolution, plants and trees have been intertwined with fungi, who made the land more inhabitable by breaking down rocks and releasing nutrients into the soil. Today, many trees and fungi engage in a mutually beneficial exchange, where the fungus receives carbon and sugars from the tree while enhancing the roots' ability to absorb water and minerals from the soil. This mycorrhizal network is a lifeline, benefiting both partners and contributing to the overall health of the ecosystem. Other fungi are saprotrophs, gorging on a tree's wood or duff. As they decompose this organic matter, they release essential nutrients back into the soil, making them available for plants and, indirectly, for animals as well. Fungi consistently establish close associations with specific types of trees, so see if you can find patterns in where and when you spot mushrooms. Each discovery is a clue to the intricate relationships that sustain our world.

Then there are the overlooked and underappreciated lichens. Commonly appearing as gray-green or yellow "mossy stuff" on tree trunks, branches, and twigs, lichens are complex symbiotic partnerships between a fungus and an alga or bacterium. Lichens don't have leaves or roots, but by clinging to tree bark or dangling from branches, they efficiently collect sunlight, moisture, and nutrients from the air. Contrary to popular belief, lichens do not harm trees. In fact, they may offer a protective shield against the elements while also providing food for animals small and large (from springtails to caribou) and nesting material for almost all hummingbirds. If you see lichens in abundance, take a big breath—their presence indicates good air quality.

ANIMALS

Pay attention, and you'll quickly realize trees are akin to a city's downtown, each one teeming with activity and their own distinct citizenry. From mammals to birds, invertebrates, reptiles, amphibians, and even fish, trees provide animals with food, habitat, shelter, and shade. Leaves can be a veritable feast. Butterfly and moth caterpillars devour foliage, often becoming a meal for birds that, in turn, help keep the caterpillar population in check. Rabbits also like

to munch upon tender spring growth after a dearth of food during the winter months. Even underground, tree roots are not spared. Insects like cicada nymphs dine on the root sap in a subterranean buffet that can last for years before their emergence to sing from the tree's crown.

Within their cavities, crevices, roots, and branches, trees supply a multitude of homes and hiding places. Birds nest in trunks and canopies while spiders weave intricate webs that catch the sunlight as it beams through. Many animals make extensive use of tree materials. Raccoons gather twigs to build dens, beavers build dams with logs, and leafcutter bees neatly cut circles from foliage to create nests. Trees are not only for work but also play. Cheerful moments can be spent climbing, swinging, and picnicking beside a tree or watching squirrels chase one another around the trunks.

Most of us are well acquainted with inhabitants like birds and squirrels, but another realm awaits when you get up close to a tree's bark. You might discover moths and cocoons camouflaged almost imperceptibly, lizards lying in wait, or maybe even a twig with appendages and antennae that moves with the gait of someone who sprained their leg—the walking stick insect.

Ants are common inhabitants spotted traversing trunks and branches, and several have evolved fascinating mutualisms with a particular tree species. Take, for example, the whistling thorn acacia, an uninviting proposition that hosts four species of stinging ants. The tree's spines, joined at the base by swollen, hollow bulbs 1 inch [2.5 cm] in diameter, resemble something once common within a medieval armory. Ants bite holes into these bulbous swellings to create nests and receive nectar from the trees in exchange for the colony's unrelenting vigilance. Like guards across a castle wall, they protect the tender leaves from other insects and the ravenous appetites of larger herbivores. Fascinatingly, when the threat of herbivores has passed, the acacia curtails the presence of ants by ceasing nectar production, revealing an independent awareness of their surroundings. Eventually, when the ants abandon these dwellings, their vacancy is announced by a whistling sound produced when air currents turn the spiky spheres into mini wind instruments.

Also be on the lookout for unusual growths called *galls*. Boasting a variety of colors, sizes, and forms, sometimes they dangle from twigs looking like small forbidden fruit, other times like an affliction of acne on the leaves. These tumor-like swellings are a tree's immune response stimulated by bacteria, fungi, mistletoes, mites, or insects. Galls are generally not harmful to healthy trees. For tiny, non-stinging cynipid wasps, galls provide food and shelter for their developing inhabitants, who in turn become food for other animals like birds. Human animals have long appreciated galls for medicine, ink, and tannins.

Nature abounds with examples of trees who have co-evolved with the animals who play an important part in their reproduction. The hues, shapes, patterns, and scents of flowers aren't merely decorative; these visual and olfactory cues are communications that attract pollinators. In these relationships of give and take, animals receive a tree's nectar and pollen. Some of that pollen gets spread around to other flowers, fertilizing them and helping ensure the next generation of trees. When we think of pollinators, bees and butterflies typically come to mind. But take a closer look; you may find birds, moths, beetles, flies, bats, geckos, and even possums doing the important work of pollination like their more heralded counterparts. And, as all manner of animals forage for delicious seeds or fruits (encasing a seed), they disperse life every time nature's call is answered or when seeds are dropped or forgotten. Observing such interactions can help us understand the far reach of a tree's influence and give us the simple joy of watching animals eat.

During mast years, when trees—including oaks, pines, and beeches—synchronize to produce copious nuts and seeds, wildlife flourishes. These bountiful periods provide crucial nourishment for animals, from birds to beetles to mammals, ensuring the survival of their young. Meanwhile, the overabundance of seeds ensures that plenty will escape the bellies of animals (with a few buried and then neglected throughout the terrain) so they can germinate into new trees.

Humans have also long relied on trees for heating, sustenance, and healing and to construct our homes, craft tools, and make art. From the olives of the ancient Levant to the cinnamon native to Sri Lanka, an abundance of foods and beverages we enjoy trace back to ingredients from trees. Hawthorn trees, whose curative properties have been known throughout the world, including in ancient China, Greece, and beyond, continue to be valued along with innumerable other medicinal trees today. With trees, we fashion everything from spoons to baskets, musical instruments, dyes, and incense. Our deep-rooted connection infuses our creativity, from physical materials like birch bark, mulberry paper, and lacquer to the inspiration for paintings, songs, and poems. In exchange, we have throughout our history tended and cultivated trees and dispersed their seeds. Nevertheless, we frequently take these gifts for granted. As you go about your day, acknowledge and give thanks for the various ways trees show up in your life—from your furniture to your utensils, cosmetics, food, and drink.

MICROBES

Many of a tree's interactions go unnoticed, but some are almost entirely invisible. Underground, in the root microbiome or *rhizosphere*, a complex community of microorganisms includes bacteria, archaea, and protozoa only viewable through a microscope. Microbes play a pivotal role in decomposing organic matter, breaking down rock, and freeing up nutrients that trees can use. In a Norwegian beech forest, a mere 2 tablespoons [30 g], of soil were found to contain *thousands* of bacteria species, exemplifying the immense diversity of the world beneath our feet.

Some symbiotic relationships between trees and bacteria become visible to us when nodules form on a tree's roots. As the bacteria receive sugars from the tree (and a protected home in the nodules), they pull nitrogen from the air and convert it into a form beneficial to the tree. You might be able to identify these nodules on trees like alders, giving them the appearance of a pustule-laden infection worthy of a zombie movie.

The dampness of forest floors and decaying leaves and wood are ideal locations for slime molds. (We've even found slime molds populating an old wooden bench in our backyard.) Though most slime molds are microscopic, plasmodial slime molds can swarm together, becoming slimy blobs, webs, or mushroom-like structures; one species of yellow slime mold is amusingly nicknamed "dog vomit." As slime molds feed on bacteria and fungi, they participate in a tree's decay and become food for beetles, slugs, and other creatures.

ESTABLISH A RELATIONSHIP

What may at first look like just "a tree" or "a log" can reveal infinite wonders when we concentrate our attention.

▶ **CHOOSE YOUR TREE**
Pick a tree (young, old, or even decaying) whom you will spend time with regularly. This should be a local tree who's easy to visit, even when life gets busy. You might be guided by your curiosity, senses, intuition, or simply proximity.

▶ **FIND YOUR FOCUS**
Which part of the tree captivates your interest? For example, the silhouette of a branch, a bud that has yet to unfurl, the way the sun or moonlight shines through the canopy, the texture of veins in the leaves, or an intriguing hollow. By concentrating on a single feature, you may become aware of interrelationships occurring,

such as water seeping into a crevice, a seed carried off.

▶ **PAY REGULAR VISITS**
Whether human or tree, getting to know someone takes time. You might revisit your tree daily (perhaps during a lunch break) or routinely throughout the seasons. The more time you can spend, the better, but visit for a little as a minute if that's all you have—the key is consistency.

▶ **RECORD AND REFLECT**
During your visits, consider documenting your observations in some way. Snap a photo, write, sketch, or make an audio recording. Think of each visit as a note; Whether your observations span a week, month, or year, by the end you will have a storied history with your tree.

Life Through Death and Decay

Even in death and decay, a tree's contribution to the ecosystem is significant and long-lasting. Fallen leaves, twigs, and other organic matter add a layer of mulch, improving water absorption, enriching the soil, filtering pollutants, and providing food and shelter for ground dwellers. This supports the health of the tree and its successor, adding to the ongoing cycle of growth and renewal.

Cavity trees and snags (standing dead trees) are critical for wildlife. Birds, mammals, reptiles, and amphibians use these woody remnants for nesting, roosting, and denning. Snags also offer foraging opportunities for birds like woodpeckers and shelter for bats and tree frogs. From our own backyard, we can spy the tops of several dead trees, giving local ravens and hawks a panoramic lookout. These snags are also popular with awkward young raptors who use them while learning how to stick a landing between flying sessions, often with varying success.

Where a tree falls, activity often arises. Under the leaf mold or within a decomposing log, you may find a kinetic calligraphy of movement, one that you might even hear when you place an ear to the ground: earthworms, snails, millipedes, woodlice, and other invertebrates, each contributing to the decomposition process as they eat and burrow. Their feasting unlocks nutrients, fortifying the soil and supporting the next generation of trees. Logs are also an excellent host for saprotrophic fungi and bacteria who break down the wood from the inside out, returning the tree's nutrients back into the ecosystem like their invertebrate counterparts.

It's not just the smallest life-forms who benefit when a tree succumbs to age, disease, or weather. Larger animals—bears, foxes, wolves, rodents, and other vertebrates—use fallen logs as woodland animal crossings, allowing them to traverse creeks, streams, and ravines. Next time you come upon a log stretched across such obstacles, look for footprints left on either side, documenting these comings and goings.

Then there are nurse logs, the rotting remains of a larger tree providing an optimal habitat for new life. Nurse logs become draped with seedlings, mosses, and other plants growing perpendicular to their prone host. Raised a few feet over the crowded, competitive forest floor, these young plants gain a foothold and advantaged access to sunlight and nutrients released during decomposition.

The decomposition of a tree can take years or even centuries, illustrating the enduring legacy of a tree's life and death. As you get to know the trees around you, pause to appreciate the ample reach of their influence and transformation. A fallen log beckons us into an accessible and rewarding opportunity to witness that a dead tree is a place of life rather than a morgue of mourning.

… TREE HUGGING

TREE LANGUAGE

Our intimate relationships with trees are conveyed by languages around the globe, with numerous words communicating what we observe across bark, branch, leaf, and root. Other words are more poetic, less precise—an attempt to convey the eddying emotions we feel when our senses are piqued by the fleeting, poignant, and elegiac.

Bulu ▶ *Dharug, Australian Aboriginal*
The shadow cast by a tree

Feuille-morte ▶ *French*
The dull yellowish or orangish brown hue of a dead or dying leaf

Hoʻolāʻau ▶ *Hawaiian*
To gather around trees, as birds or people; to persist and form mature wood

Komorebi ▶ *Japanese*
The shimmering and ephemeral dance of sunlight filtered through the canopy of trees

Waldeinsamkeit ▶ *German*
The melancholic feeling of solitude in the woods

What if you were
a great teacher,
a holder of KNOWLEDGE
and vessel of STORIES,
but had no audible voice
with which to speak?...
Plants tell their STORIES
not by what they say
but by WHAT THEY DO.

—Robin Wall Kimmerer, from *"White Pine"*

III.

THE WISDOM OF TREES

The wisdom we seek from trees is unique. Recognizing them as our fellow living counterparts, they become a natural canvas for humankind to paint a sweeping range of emotions, thoughts, hopes, and fears. As we've built relationships with trees, they have nourished, sheltered, and healed us. We have been inspired by their beauty and turned to them for solace. In their wizened bark and changing leaves, we see the literal weathering of storms and passing of seasons, and in their gnarled roots reaching into the depths, we recognize our own unseeable struggles reflected. Their enduring presence spans generations—ours and their own.

It is no surprise then that across continents, cultures, and time periods, people have regarded trees as arboreal mentors. The powerful symbolism of trees appears in countless creation stories and spiritual and philosophical traditions. Throughout the world, sacred trees, trees of life, and tree spirits have been and continue to be venerated. The oldest picture of a tree, painted upon the cave walls at the Serra da Capivara National Park in Brazil, seems to depict our early ancestors festively dancing around or maybe even worshipping a tree.

In thirteenth-century Norse sagas, Yggdrasil, an ash tree of universal proportions, was believed to encase all of existence. Origin stories of the Hadza in Tanzania describe how the first people climbed down to Earth from a baobab tree (ʄ//oba-ko) or were born inside the trunk. A white pine, known as the Great Tree of Peace (Skaęhetsi'kona), plays a pivotal role for the Haudenosaunee Confederacy; under the tree's canopy, five Indigenous nations came together. And since antiquity, branches of sakaki trees planted at Japanese

Shinto shrines have been crafted into offerings to kami (spirits) and used in ritual dances, purification rites, and as decorations to designate a sacred space. These are only a few of the innumerable stories from which humankind and trees have intertwined.

On the following pages are some of the things we have learned from trees. As you build your own kinships with trees and listen to the stories they share, you will surely have other insights to add.

PERSPECTIVES

Spending one-on-one time with a tree invites us to adopt a beginner's mind as we trace the curve of a branch, peer into the crevice of a knotty trunk, listen to the call of a bird perched high above, or marvel at the glimmer of sunlight dancing through leaves. Intermediaries between soil and sky, they stitch together our impressions of the world above and below ground, seen and unseen.

Unlike most animals, trees seem practically motionless. Slowing down to "tree time" can grant us something so many of us deeply crave: an affirming respite from the relentless pace of modern life. Imagine the rustle of leaves versus the compounding stress of phone notifications. Being with a tree can anchor us firmly in the present by simply stopping, sensing, and feeling.

At the same moment, a tree stands as a living testament to the past. Many trees live on a time scale far beyond our own. Contemplating all they have witnessed over hundreds or

TREE HUGGING

even thousands of years enriches our appreciation of time and place. The imprint of history, evolution, ancestors, geology, climate, weather, and whoever planted their seed, whether human, blue jay, or wind current—each tree holds these stories within their very being. Coupled with this is the fact that trees often outlive us. A tree is at once an incarnation of physical and temporal past, present, and future.

When we observe closely, we realize a tree is not only a tree. They are also the embodiment of the energy of the sun and fire; the nourishment of the earth, minerals, and water; and the cycles of air. This community of connections exists from the understory to the overstory, beneath the soil's surface and up toward the clouds. A tree sculpts and is sculpted by the land and the diversity of microbes, fungi, plants, and animals whose lives are intertwined. Giving our attention to this interwoven web of relationships can expand our care for trees and all beings.

Despite our tendency to anthropomorphize them, trees are radically different from us. As we get to know a tree using our senses, we might recognize that our perceptions are subjective. Just as a human experiences the world differently from a dog or another human, a tree interprets their environment through senses uniquely their own. It may not be possible for us to truly understand how a tree experiences life, from how their roots relate to the soil to how they perceive a woodpecker's tap or communicate with other trees. But this should not preclude our empathy. Might we simply embrace a humility rooted in that unknowing, in the ways trees are not like us, and still feel the wonder of it all?

TREE HUGGING

YOUR TREE-FFS

World-famous trees often attract the spotlight for being spectacularly old, large, or otherwise extraordinary. People travel long distances to visit those trees, perhaps engaging little beyond snapping a photo and checking the item off their "nature tourism bucket list." Local trees often get cast to the wayside. To remedy this, let's cultivate a reverence for the trees who live close to home!

Make a list of local trees you'd like to share with a loved one. These might be trees you interact with or tend to or who have special meaning in your life—the ones you like to sit and sleep beneath, whose leaves or bark fascinate you, or whom you feel compelled to greet on your walks, like an old friend.

ROOTEDNESS

As sentinels of time and the landscape, trees offer a reassuring sense of place. This becomes particularly evident when we follow the path from a tree's trunk down to their roots, into the ground until completely unseen. A tree's bond with the Earth defines their very being throughout the entirety of their life.

A tree exists as their own being, but also a gathering place, a landmark, and a beacon that helps us navigate both the physical realm and the intricacies of our existence. When we hurry through life and speed by in cars, trains, and planes, it can be hard to truly grasp the fullness of where we are. But when we find ourselves spending a moment with a tree and connecting with a life that is rooted to the ground, it can help us feel steady and supported. Being in the company of a tree allows us to stamp our passports with *here and now*.

In the tapestry of the world, each tree is a distinctive thread, woven from the very soil that moors their roots. And in their steadfast growth, the tree also weaves the air we breathe, the land we tread, and the myriad lives who receive their gifts. Humans today tend to overlook our threads within this fabric, forgetting that we are as much a part of Earth as the trees. "Nature" is not a distant entity, separate from our daily lives or bodies. Although our roots grow differently, trees remind us that we too are inextricable from our surroundings. From this grounding, we draw a special sustenance and, like the trees, can be more open to what Mary Oliver described in *Long Life* as "a sudden awareness of the citizenry of all things within one world."

RESILIENCE

We tend to view trees as unchanging. In reality, they exemplify adaptability, ephemerality, and potential. From moment to moment, trees adjust to what is needed, and each tree grows into a unique form that speaks to their resilience. Roots wrap around rocks and travel to mine water and nutrients, trunks arch toward the sun, branches recover from storms, and leaves grow broader to soak up light. Trees who have evolved for cold climates prepare themselves for winter and then awaken in the spring. Those who endure fires, freezes, or droughts often surprise us by sprouting after we thought them gone.

A tree's rhythms encompass the large and small, from the daily flow of water and nutrients, photosynthesis, and transpiration; to annual and seasonal patterns; to a lifetime that encompasses growth, decay, and renewal. Across the seasons and the life of a tree, we watch a multitude of moments unfold: the potential of a seed, the vigor of unfurling leaves, the brilliance of a flower that turns into ripe fruit, the letting go of leaves, the slowing down of an aging tree. With time and the aid of the elements alongside the efforts of other organisms, a fallen log will return to the soil, nourishing new trees. Water, minerals, air, and light continuously circulate through the tree's life processes, as they do through our own bodies. Birth and death are not discontinuous; each phase nurtures and balances the other.

As we encounter these cycles, we can understand that life is ever-changing and dynamic and thus learn to embrace unpredictable moments. We can also find inspiration to live in harmony with the seasons. For example, what do you observe in the world around and within you as sunlight, moisture, or temperature shift throughout the year? Like a tree, is your energy in a phase of growth, expression, or rest? When we align our rhythms with our environment and our internal needs, we can feel a deeper sense of resilience, connection, and flow. Trees also show us that the capacity for resilience is strengthened by community, just as a tree is supported by fungi, pollinators, and the entirety of the landscape.

HEALTH BENEFITS

Have you ever noticed the difference in how you feel when you're in a forest or park versus a place absent of plants or trees? In natural as well as built landscapes, trees positively affect our mental and physical well-being. A walk in the woods or a lunch break beneath a tree can leave us feeling refreshed and restored. This type of experience is so therapeutic that in Japan, *shinrin-yoku*, or forest bathing, is recognized as a kind of healthcare. Like bathing in a tub immerses us in water, forest bathing immerses us in the atmosphere of the trees. At its simplest, the practice involves engaging one's senses while walking mindfully through a forest. Other forest therapy practices include lying in a hammock, visiting hot springs, and eating or drinking tea in the forest.

Many of us take nutritional supplements or multivitamins as a preventive measure, even though we may feel unsure if they're really doing us any good. But time spent amongst trees—under swaying palms at the coast, beneath the shade of desert trees, or surrounded by the spectacle of autumn leaves—is almost always perceived as therapeutic and reinvigorating. Since the formal introduction of shinrin-yoku in 1982, numerous scientific studies have confirmed that forest bathing has remarkable physiological and psychological benefits, including improved immunity and sleep; increased relaxation and energy; reduced stress, anxiety, and depression; and lowered blood pressure.

Researchers of shinrin-yoku posit that mindfully engaging with a forest, or even a simple potted plant, can help regulate the nervous system as our own rhythms (re)-synchronize with those of the environment. This is especially crucial in our modern society, where we spend an inordinate amount of time indoors apart from the rest of the natural world, a separation made worse by the stressors of commuting and staring at screens. Scientists have also discovered that organic compounds released by certain trees, particularly evergreens, can improve mood and overall well-being—a type of aromatherapy. It's often said that seeing is believing, but the scent of trees reveals another layer of perception—one that becomes apparent when we take it all in using a combination of the senses available to us, such as sight, smell, sound, touch, and even taste.

Although these studies provide compelling validation, many of us intuitively understand the restorative benefits of being in the company of trees. And these good feelings are not limited to forests alone. One might also experience tranquility, comfort, and meaning while spending time in a city park or local botanical garden or under a backyard tree.

So, it is well established that trees are good for us as individuals, but their contributions to health extend to our communities and even globally. As they create shade and emit oxygen and water vapor, trees improve our air quality and help cool our buildings and cities. They also absorb carbon dioxide from the air and lock up carbon within their wood and in the soil. How much carbon dioxide a tree can sequester is hard to pin down and varies between species, but it's thought that a mature tree may be able to sequester as much as 48 pounds [22 kg], possibly more, of carbon dioxide annually. Because trees are vital to the welfare of humans and countless other beings, it's imperative we consider them a critical ally in our battle against the effects of climate change.

RECIPROCITY

When you recall your most important and lasting relationships, what do you think of? There's a strong likelihood they've flourished from the soil of reciprocity—a mutually beneficial exchange in which each party recognizes life is better together than apart. Such an interconnected bond compels us to adopt a higher degree of responsibility and care when we understand our and others' health is intertwined.

Trees may be resilient, but their survival will undoubtedly require our aid. Globally, trees and their ecosystems are facing mounting odds, imperiled by climate change, deforestation, and forest fragmentation driven by development, suburban sprawl, mining, oil drilling, and agriculture. Climate shifts are happening on such a rapid scale that it can be difficult for trees to withstand the extreme temperatures and intensity of droughts, floods, and fires alongside weakened resistance to

MOVE WITH TREES

Inspired by shinrin-yoku and walking meditation, this practice can be done in a park or forest, city green space, backyard, arboretum—anywhere there are trees. Reaching a destination isn't your goal. Whether you spend ten minutes or two hours, this activity is most beneficial when you are able to be fully present.

▶ **FIND A SPACE**
Choose someplace you feel safe and can move comfortably on foot, by wheelchair or other mobility device, or any way you are able. This shouldn't be a strenuous hike. You can also modify this exercise for sitting or standing in place or even looking out a window.

▶ **BEGIN YOUR STROLL**
If possible, switch off your phone so you can be immersed in the present. Go at a leisurely pace, taking your time and moving without hurry or aim.

- **BRING AWARENESS TO YOUR BODY**
  For example, pay attention to your feet or wheels making contact with the ground, the sensation of your body in your seat, the movement of your hands, the flow of your breath, or the air on your skin. Respond to the multidimensionality of a tree by raising your arms to the sky, outlining a flower with your fingers, or mimicking the bend of a branch.

- **EXPERIENCE YOUR SURROUNDINGS**
  Using your senses, drink in the atmosphere: perhaps birds and insects singing, cool shade cast by trees, the scent of damp soil, or whatever you notice. (You might do a variation of the exercise on pages 38 and 39.)

- **PAUSE FROM TIME TO TIME**
  If your interest is drawn to a beam of sunlight or a snail crawling across a leaf, simply appreciate the moment. Hug a tree or lean against a trunk if you are beckoned!

Remember, the intention is to feel relaxed and refreshed, so heed your own experiences and adjust this activity as desired.

disease and insects. For example, California coast live oaks have evolved a thick, furrowed layer of bark that allows them to withstand frequent, low-intensity wildfires that were once a normal occurrence of the local ecology. It's not uncommon to see a lone oak survivor standing practically unscathed in the apocalyptic aftermath of a wildfire. Even when an oak is burned to an unrecognizable char, their roots can survive to shoot out the promise of a better tomorrow. But with fires now raging hotter and more frequently, even this arboreal phoenix can succumb to the flames and never reemerge.

So what can you do today to give back to trees? The answer is not one-size-fits-all. Each ecosystem is unique, and the needs of your particular location will vary. Your support for trees could come in the form of caring for existing trees, planting new ones, or advocating for their protection. Humans aren't doomed to destroy, and our ancestral ways can help steward the future. Around the planet, Indigenous communities have long held expertise in nurturing biodiversity and reciprocity through tending, harvesting, and land management practices. Locate people and groups in your area who are already looking after the trees and ask how you can collaborate. As observing trees teaches us, working together, connected in community, makes us stronger.

Planting a tree can feel rewarding, an act that can positively affect not only your life but future generations. However, before you start digging a hole, give thought to which species you are planting. Even a tree native to your area needs proper growing conditions to flourish. Consider the mantra *right tree, right place, right care*. For the best chance of helping a tree thrive, you should find out what kind of soil, water, sun, and space they need. Also contemplate how the tree will become part of the fabric of your community—both human and nonhuman—over time.

While saplings evoke promise, it is equally, if not more, important to care for mature trees and forests. Find out what you can do to preserve and care for the trees already in your midst: in yards, parks, undeveloped areas, or elsewhere. We tend to mourn after a tree dies or is chopped down, but let's remember to care for the trees while they're here, living alongside us. Potential avenues of caregiving include leaving the fallen leaves in your yard to enrich the soil, working with arborists to ensure trees are structurally sound, and becoming aware of local actions to protect trees and their relationships with other plants, animals, and fungi. To be a good steward of trees farther from home, when buying tree-based products, support makers who tend and harvest using regenerative practices.

What about widespread tree planting initiatives or projects that plant trees to offset carbon emissions? These can be worthwhile, but many times they result in monocultures of trees lacking the richness of a true forest. Thriving and healthy ecosystems are characterized by biodiversity and interconnectedness. And beyond the initial planting, those projects may not have a plan to care for the trees as they mature.

PARTING WORDS

We often believe a meaningful kinship between us and our wooded counterparts necessitates a journey to some distant forest or a pilgrimage seeking the counsel of a revered, prehistoric tree covered in gnarled bark. It is our nature to seek wisdom from the ancient and be impressed by the grandiose. But in the process, it can be easy to ignore the knowledge right in our yards, lining our streets, shading our parks, and everywhere we've planted trees in our conscious and unconscious desire to be in their presence. Whether local or far away, trees are not only worthy of our affection but now more than ever require our protection. As the world faces unprecedented environmental challenges, the permanence of our beloved trees can no longer be taken for granted. These once-enduring symbols of resilience are now endangered because of the effects of climate change, deforestation, and urban expansion. Yet, there remains a hopefulness, one rooted in the belief that our attention can plant the seeds of action.

Remember, trees are more than mere backdrops; they are givers of life and markers of our collective and individual histories. They are often figuratively, sometimes physically, living archives written across the sky, leaf by leaf, and beneath the soil in the cursive of roots. The significance of trees can be immensely personal, entwined with our lives in moments of both joy and sorrow. In the refuge of trees, we rest and play, acknowledge our love and grief, and find continuity by commemorating births, unions, and deaths.

When Gregory was a child, his mother planted a small mimosa tree, a memory he was told more than remembers. The tree's growth ran parallel to his own from adolescence into adulthood, first ensconced against a backyard wall with the disinterested posture of a teen. Propped such, the mimosa matured into a towering, verdant expression of fern-like leaves, their crown covered in a confetti of dazzling blooms, miniature pink and white fireworks frozen in time. These flowers attracted bees, butterflies, ants, and most conspicuously, a whir of hummingbirds vying to stake claim to the tree's nectar. Later, that same nectar was gathered by Emily to make herbal elixirs that lift the spirits. We still occasionally think of the spillage of shade beneath the mimosa, where Mom would sit during summer sunsets, contentedly observing the comings and goings in her corner of this world.

Today, Gregory's mom and dad rest together side by side under a magnolia tree, with large white blooms that perfume the air with love and melancholy. Similarly, we buried our cat Eames, who lived to the ripe age of twenty-one, under a young oak tree. We like to imagine his spirit now infuses the oak and will compel the tree to grow into someone as grand as our memories of him. Our other beloved feline, Eero, has found her place of remembrance beneath a resplendent old oak in our front yard. We should all be so lucky to return to the earth in the intimate company of trees.

RESOURCES

Farmer, Jared. *Elderflora: A Modern History of Ancient Trees*. New York: Basic Books, 2022.

Hesse, Hermann. *Trees: An Anthology of Writings and Paintings*. Edited by Volker Michels. Translated by Damion Searls. San Diego: Kales Press, 2022.

Holten, Katie. *The Language of Trees: A Rewilding of Literature and Landscape*. Portland, OR: Tin House, 2023.

Kimmerer, Robin Wall. *Braiding Sweetgrass: Indigenous Wisdom, Scientific Knowledge, and the Teachings of Plants*. Minneapolis: Milkweed Editions, 2013.

Li, Qing. *Forest Bathing: How Trees Can Help You Find Health and Happiness*. New York: Viking, 2018.

Miyazaki, Yoshifumi. *Walking in the Woods: Go Back to Nature with the Japanese Way of Shinrin-Yoku*. London: Aster, 2021.

Nadkarni, Nalini M. *Between Earth and Sky: Our Intimate Connections to Trees*. Berkeley: University of California Press, 2008.

Nassar, Dalia, and Margaret Barbour. "Rooted," *Aeon*, October 16, 2019, https://aeon.co/essays/what-can-an-embodied-history-of-trees-teach-us-about-life.

Nhất Hạnh, Thích. *A Guide to Walking Meditation*. Nyack, NY: Fellowship Publications, 1985.

Thomas, Peter A. *Trees: Their Natural History*. 2nd ed. Cambridge: Cambridge University Press, 2014.

CREDITS

Kobayashi Issa, ["cheerful cheerful"], translated by Stephen Addiss, from *The Art of Haiku: Its History Through Poems and Paintings by Japanese Masters*. Copyright © 2012 by Stephen Addiss. Reprinted by arrangement with The Permissions Company, LLC on behalf of Shambhala Publications, Inc., shambhala.com.

Excerpt(s) from *The Songs of Trees: From Nature's Great Connectors* by David George Haskell, copyright © 2017 by David George Haskell. Used by permission of Viking Books, an imprint of Penguin Publishing Group, a division of Penguin Random House LLC. All rights reserved.

Robin Wall Kimmerer, excerpt from "White Pine" from *The Mind of Plants: Narratives of Vegetal Intelligence*. Copyright © by John C. Ryan, Patrícia Vieira, and Monica Gagliano. Reprinted with the permission of Synergetic Press, Santa Fe, NM.

GREGORY HAN is a trail-seeker and writer for *Dwell*, *Design Milk*, and *Wirecutter*. He is the coauthor of *Creative Spaces: People, Homes, and Studios to Inspire* and *Pocket Nature: Mushroom Hunting*.

EMILY HAN is a naturalist, herbalist, and educator. She is the author of *Wild Drinks and Cocktails* and coauthor of *Wild Remedies* and *Pocket Nature: Mushroom Hunting*.

THE POCKET NATURE SERIES offers meditative and insightful guides to reconnecting with the natural world through mindful practices.

SEE MORE BOOKS IN THE SERIES

WWW.CHRONICLEBOOKS.COM/POCKETNATURE